Secrets
of the
Bible

Timothy J. Dailey, PhD

Consultant:
David M. Howard Jr., PhD

Publications International, Ltd.

Author: Timothy J. Dailey earned his doctorate in theology from Marquette University. He has taught biblical history in the United States and Israel.

Contributing author: David M. Howard Jr.

Consultant: David M. Howard Jr. holds a PhD in Near Eastern Studies from the University of Michigan. He is the author of *Fascinating Bible Facts.*

Editorial assistance: Loren D. Lineberry

Picture Credits: Dover, Jupiterimages

ISBN-13: 978-1-4508-7281-2
ISBN-10: 1-4508-7281-6

Manufactured in China.

8 7 6 5 4 3 2 1

Contents

About the Bible

he first part of the Bible is made up of 39 books. Tradition holds that Ezra compiled these books, but this cannot be proven.

"Old Testament" is a misnomer. It implies that a "New Testament" follows, which, of course, did not happen for more than 1,500 years. Today, it is called the Old Testament only when referring to the first part of the Christian Bible. When referring to the text used by the Jewish religion, "Hebrew scriptures" is the generally accepted term.

The New Testament consists of the four Gospels, the Acts of the Apostles, letters written by Paul and other apostles, and Revelation.

Secrets of the Bible elaborates on many of the Bible's mysteries, providing reasonable explanations for some. For others, it provides theories about what may be behind the secrets.

Whether you are familiar with the scriptures or are simply intrigued by the "unknowns" that inundate our universe, the many mysteries contained in the following pages are sure to intrigue you.

The Tree of Knowledge

he Garden of Eden was a place of unimaginable beauty, prepared by God specifically for human beings to enjoy. It had trees that were "pleasant to the sight and good for food" (Genesis 2:9), it was watered well by four rivers, and it abounded in precious metals and stones.

God expressed his generosity to Adam in the following way: "Of every tree of the garden you may freely eat" (Genesis 2:16). The only exception was that Adam was not to eat of the tree of knowledge of good and evil. In fact, there

Expulsion from the Garden of Eden

were two special trees in the garden: the tree of knowledge of good and evil and the tree of life. The tree of life is mentioned elsewhere in the Bible, but its role in the Garden of Eden was minimal; the tree of knowledge is the significant one here.

Scholars have long debated the significance of this tree and its forbidden fruit. One theory is that the tree represents

Even though an apple is commonly thought to be what Adam and Eve ate, the Bible does not actually specify what the fruit was.

moral autonomy—that is, the human desire to live apart from God. Humans were created in God's image, and he provided for all of their needs. They were meant to live in close relationship with him. Sadly, when Adam and Eve sinned, this relationship was broken, and they hid themselves from God.

When God prohibited Adam and Eve from eating of this tree, he was underscoring the fact that he wanted to be their God and their provider. When they violated his command, they became in a sense "like God" (Genesis 3:5); but this was a burden they could not handle, since their created

purpose was to live in total dependence on him.
For this denial of their dependence on God, Adam
and Eve were driven out of the Garden of Eden.

The Great Flood

he Bible tells us that just ten genera-
tions after the creation of Adam and Eve,
the wickedness of their descendants was
such that "the Lord was sorry that he had made
man on the earth, and he was grieved in his heart"
(Genesis 6:6). Summoning the rain, he decided to
destroy humankind with a massive flood so that he
could start all over again.

The Lord found an exception in righteous
Noah, deciding to spare him and his family, along
with the animals and other living creatures. The
ark Noah was instructed to build was actually a
huge wooden barge. With a length of 450 feet, a
width of 75 feet, and three interior decks reaching
a height of 45 feet, it would have been the largest

seagoing vessel known before the 20th century. Interestingly, its dimensions are remarkably similar to that of some modern ships.

Scholars are divided as to the extent of the biblical flood, many holding that it may have

been a local event limited to the Mesopotamian floodplain. The Bible, however, is unequivocal in stating that "the waters prevailed exceedingly upon the earth; and all the

Noah building the ark

high hills, that were under the whole heaven, were covered" (Genesis 7:19).

Archaeologists have attempted to find evidence of such a flood in Mesopotamia. Their efforts have thus far proved inconclusive.

In 1872, the scholarly world was rocked by the publication of the contents of a cuneiform tablet from Nineveh on which was written a Babylonian account of a great flood. The text is part of the Epic of Gilgamesh, an ancient epic poem of Mesopotamia. In part of the story, the hero Utnapishtim of Shuruppak is warned that Enlil, the chief god of the Babylonian pantheon, would soon destroy humankind with a flood. Utnapishtim was instructed to build an ark for himself and his family and "the seeds of all living things."

Unlike the biblical account of Noah's flood, in which the rains and floods continued for 40 days and nights, the floods in the Epic of Gilgamesh lasted only six days and nights.

Utnapishtim and his ark also come to rest on a mountaintop. Like his biblical counterpart, Utnapishtim opens a window and releases a series of birds to find out if the surface of the earth has dried sufficiently. In yet another parallel, Utnapishtim's first act upon leaving the ark is to build an altar and offer a sacrifice. Since the discovery of the flood story in the Epic of Gilgamesh, at least two other Mesopotamian flood stories have come to light, both containing the same central features.

Since then, scholars have pondered the relationship between the Mesopotamian flood stories and the biblical narrative. Some have suggested that all of these accounts refer to the same flood. If so, then we should expect to find flood stories in other ancient cultures in other parts of the world. And this is exactly what ethnologists have discovered. James Frazer, a well-known student of religions around the world, has collected many flood stories from places as diverse as Greece, the South Pacific, and the Americas. Such evidence presents at least the possibility that a worldwide flood of cataclysmic proportions occurred.

Abraham in History

he age of the biblical patriarchs remains shrouded in mystery. Some scholars believe that Abraham, Isaac, Jacob, and Joseph existed only in the pious imaginations of later Hebrew writers. Those who believe that the patriarchs are rooted in history say it is unreasonable to expect sources beyond the Bible to confirm events in the life of Abraham. The fact that a tent-dweller such as Abraham figures prominently in the Bible does not mean he merits attention in ancient Near Eastern historical records.

However, archaeologists have uncovered what some believe is a reference to the Hebrew patriarch in a nonbiblical record. It comes from the reign of Pharaoh Sheshonq I, whom many scholars equate with the biblical Shishak.

In the Book of 1 Kings we read of a campaign against Palestine by Shishak: "And it came to pass in the fifth year of king Rehoboam, that Shishak king of Egypt came up against Jerusalem . . . and he took away all the shields of gold which Solomon had made" (1 Kings 14:25–26).

If Pharaoh Sheshonq is to be equated with the biblical Shishak—and scholars are not agreed on this—we have an interesting parallel in an inscription in the Temple of Amun in Karnak. Throughout Egyptian history, whenever pharaohs returned from a victorious military campaign, they would record their triumph for posterity. At Karnak, archaeologists have deciphered a stela, or standing stone, on which Pharaoh Sheshonq describes his triumphant campaign against Israel.

Most of the perhaps 150 names on the stela are unreadable. Of those that remain, perhaps 70 names come from the Negev, a desert in southern Israel. One of those has been identified by Egyptologists as the equivalent of the Hebrew "Abram." The phrase where the name occurs reads: "The fort [or fortified town] of Abraham."

Among all the books of the Bible, Genesis covers the broadest span of time (from Creation to the second millennium B.C.) and space (from Iraq to Egypt and beyond).

Is the "Abram" of Fort Abram the biblical patriarch? Possibly. The biblical Abraham lived in the Negev where this "Fort Abram" was located. Such an outpost may have been built in the time of David or Solomon as part of a line of fortifications against Egyptian intrusion. It would not be unusual for the fort to be named after some national hero or revered personage such as the patriarch.

Other scholars suggest that Fort Abram is actually Beersheba, a city founded by Abraham (Genesis 21:32–33). The reason behind this notion is that Beersheba is not mentioned elsewhere in Pharaoh Sheshonq's list. Since it was a prominent city in the Negev, its omission is unexplainable, unless, perhaps, it is the very same city called Fort Abram by the Egyptians.

If so, the connection with the biblical patriarch becomes probable, and it constitutes evidence that Abraham was a real person who lived in the memory—and in the place names—of the ancient Hebrews.

Israel's Ancient Enemy

n the Negev desert of southern Israel are many Israelite fortresses that puzzled archaeologists for some time. What enemy were these military installations designed to protect against? Recent evidence indicates that they were a frontline defense against Edom, Israel's ancient enemy.

The story of Jacob and Esau is one of sibling rivalry that foreshadows the continuing strife in the Middle East. While the two brothers were still in the womb of Rebekah, the Lord said to her:

"Two nations are in thy womb,
and two manner of people shall be separated
from thy bowels;
and the one shall be stronger than the other
people;
and the elder shall serve the younger."
—(Genesis 25:23)

Esau, the firstborn, was tricked by his brother Jacob into surrendering his birthright for a serving of stew. Then, with Rebekah's connivance, Jacob deceived Isaac, his dying father, into giving him the blessing usually reserved for the firstborn son. Eventually, Esau took Canaanite wives and settled in the hill country of what today is southern Jordan—but which was then known as Edom.

Until recently, little was known of the nation that figured so prominently in Israel's early history.

Herod the Great's Connection to Edom

Edom was destined to fade from history, but not before making its mark once more in the form of one of its most infamous descendants. By the fourth century B.C., the Edomites in the Negev were called by another name: Idumeans. The father of Herod the Great was an Idumean who married a Nabataean. And so the two peoples were symbolically united in the turbulent person of Herod, a ruler legendary for his cruelty and insecurity.

It was the Edomites who, despite assurances by the Israelites, refused to allow them to pass through their territory on their way to the Promised Land. The route that the Israelites desired to take was an ancient trade route known as the King's Highway. Edom would later pay dearly for its hostility when it was attacked by King Saul and conquered by King David.

Archaeologists were surprised to discover evidence of Edomite cities in the Negev region of southern Israel. Some scholars think these cities date to the seventh century B.C., a time of political upheaval in Judea. The northern kingdom of Israel had fallen to the Assyrians, and the Babylonians were encroaching ever deeper into the southern kingdom of Judea.

The large number of ritual artifacts—including idols, incense altars, and cultic shrines—uncovered at the Edomite sites reflect the profusion of deities that the populace worshipped. Their polytheistic practices stand in marked contrast to the strict monotheism of the Israelite nation. The considerable religious and cultural differences between the two groups ensured that they would remain perpetually at odds, and it could possibly explain the reason for the line of Judean forts in the Negev.

☙—❧

The Death of Rachel

 acob saw the lovely Rachel bringing her sheep to water and was instantly smitten. He would work seven years for her father, Laban, for the right to marry her, followed by another seven years because of Laban's craftiness in tricking him.

The love they shared was made even more touching by the untimely death of Rachel during childbirth. From that time on, it is clear that Jacob favored Joseph and Benjamin, the two sons that Rachel bore him. When he is shown Joseph's bloody coat and believes him to be dead, Jacob is inconsolable. Later, he takes the unusual step of granting Joseph's two sons, Ephraim and Manasseh, equal inheritance rights to that of his own sons.

Jacob explains why he is doing this: "... when I came from Padan, Rachel died beside me in the land of Canaan on the way" (Genesis 48:7). Until the end of his life, Jacob was haunted by the death of his beloved Rachel. A startling reason has been suggested as to why Jacob was so troubled: He felt responsible.

To understand this, we must return to when Jacob and Rachel finally took their leave of Laban and set out for Canaan. Before they left, Rachel took her father's household idols (probably because she thought they would bring good luck). When he discovered that his idols were gone, Laban pursued Jacob and accused him of the theft. Unaware that his beloved wife had taken the idols, an indignant Jacob vowed that "With whomever you find your gods, do not let him live" (Genesis 31:32).

Oaths were considered binding in biblical times, and they often had unintended effects. By pronouncing judgment upon the guilty—even though Jacob was ignorant of Rachel's action—he unwittingly

Rachel and Jacob

condemned her to death. Rachel herself was unaware of Jacob's oath. While he was speaking with Laban, she was in her tent, guarding the idols by sitting on them.

After leaving Laban, Jacob was commanded by the Lord to go to Bethel and build an altar. Bethel was an important religious site for the Hebrew patriarchs: It was here that Abraham "called on the name of the Lord" (Genesis 12:8). Jacob had stopped at Bethel many years earlier on his flight from his brother Esau. During that night, he dreamed of a ladder going up to heaven. The Lord spoke to him, confirming the blessing originally given to Abraham.

In preparing for his arrival at the holy site of Bethel, Jacob instructed his family and servants: "Put away the foreign gods that are among you, purify yourselves, and change your garments. Then let us arise and go up to Bethel" (Genesis 35:2–3). It was likely he did not suspect Rachel had idols in her possession.

The text does not say that Rachel surrendered her idols at Jacob's command, though it is reasonable to conclude that she did. The text states that the people with him "gave Jacob all the foreign gods which were in their hands" (Genesis 35:4). Rachel likely complied with the others, not having heard Jacob's fateful oath to Laban and being unaware of any consequences that would follow.

But the tragic consequences would follow all too soon. Doubtless with a heavy heart, Jacob left Bethel with his family. They did not get far, for we read that Rachel went into labor and died giving birth to her son Benjamin. And so Jacob buried her and went on his way, perhaps tormented by the fear that his hastily spoken oath may have been Rachel's death sentence.

The Red Sea

 ew events recorded in the Bible capture the imagination like the story of Moses parting the Red Sea. Many contemporary Americans associate this event with the image of actor Charlton Heston raising his staff over the waters in *The Ten Commandments,* the epic 1956 Cecil B. DeMille film.

Biblical scholars are divided about this event. Did the Children of Israel cross a body of water that miraculously parted for them—or was it actually a marsh they crossed, which providentially happened to ensnare the chariots of the pursuing Egyptians?

Part of the mystery involves the identification of the Hebrew words *yam suf,* which are translated in some versions of the Bible as "Red Sea." Scholars have long known that the word "red" is not indicated by the words *yam suf.* A better translation of the Hebrew words would be "Reed Sea"—a reading that opens the possibility that the Israelites crossed a swampy area to the north of the Red Sea. Accordingly, many historical maps trace the route of the Exodus through the marshy Lake Timsah or Bitter Lake region.

This solution is not as simple as it seems. It cannot be denied that some biblical references to *yam suf* clearly refer to the Red Sea. Complicating the problem is the fact that the parting of the Red Sea is not mentioned in any contemporary Egyptian texts. Some have taken this as evidence that the event is mythological rather than historical. Yet the omission is not surprising.

The royal chronicles of ancient times were notorious for ignoring events that might cast the ruler in an unfavorable light. It would be hard to imagine any ancient ruler chronicling the loss of an entire army in pursuit of a mass exodus of unarmed slaves.

Water from a Rock?

he Bible says that when the Israelites arrived at Rephidim, there was no water available to them. This may have been because the Amalekites controlled the only spring in the area and were jealous to protect it.

The disgruntled Israelites demanded water from Moses. We then read of a curious action on Moses' part. He was commanded by the Lord to take his rod and go to the rock of Horeb: "I will stand before you there on the rock in Horeb; and you shall strike the rock, and water will come out of it, that the people may drink" (Exodus 17:6).

While this action may be unimaginable to the modern mind, bedouin people of times past or present would realize exactly what happened. In the desert wadis of the Sinai, the scarce rainfall filters down and collects in porous layers of lime-stone. These layers are exposed at the base of the moun-tains, but just as water deposits can

Moses obtains water from a rock

eventually clog a faucet, the water cannot escape because of a thick buildup of limestone crust. Bedouin know precisely how to look for these hidden water sources.

There are accounts of this phenomenon in recent times. In the 1930s, Major C. S. Jarvis, the British Governor of the Sinai, was leading a camel expedition through a dry wadi when his men came across a trickle of water coming out of the lime-stone rock. Trying to dig into the ground where he thought there might be a pool of water, one of his men struck the rock by mistake. To everyone's surprise and delight, the hard crust fell away and out of the crevice shot a powerful stream of water.

This method of obtaining water was employed by Moses on at least one other occasion. We read that on the journey from Kadesh to Edom "Moses lifted his hand and struck the rock twice with his rod; and water came out abundantly, and the congregation and their animals drank" (Numbers 20:11). On this occasion, Moses disobeyed by striking the rock instead of speaking to it as the Lord had commanded.

We can only speculate that the Israelites had by then learned of this means of obtaining water in the desert. Perhaps God had intended to perform a miracle by having Moses speak to the rock instead of strike it. In any event, Moses' disobedience at Kadesh cost him dearly. He was denied the opportunity to personally lead the children of Israel into the Promised Land.

The Presence of God

he ark of the covenant was an elaborate container that symbolized God's presence among the ancient Israelites.

The Hebrew word for "ark" can be used interchangeably to mean "box," "chest," or "coffin" and was used to describe objects as diverse as the coffin of Joseph and the collection box in the temple. The word "covenant" refers to the original purpose of the ark as a container for the Ten Commandments.

The ark was constructed while the Israelites resided at Mount Sinai. After Moses broke the original tablets of the law because of the Israelites' idolatry, he made the ark as a container for the new tablets. Constructed out of acacia wood and overlaid with gold, the ark was a rectangular-shaped box approximately four feet long, two-and-a-half feet wide, and two-and-a-half feet deep. It had built-in handles and was carried only by priests.

During the wanderings of the Israelites, the ark was kept within the tabernacle. Moses addressed the ark as if the divine presence were within:

"So it was, whenever the ark set out, that Moses said: 'Rise up, O Lord! Let Your enemies be scattered, And let those who hate You flee before You.' And when it rested, he said: 'Return, O Lord, To the many thousands of Israel'" (Numbers 10:35–36).

As the powerful symbol of God's presence, the ark was routinely taken into battle. During the period of the Judges, the sin of the wicked sons of Eli led to the defeat of the Israelites

The ark of the covenant

by the Philistines. The ark was captured by the Israelites' mortal enemies.

This led to a series of adventures in which the ark was passed from one Philistine city to another, bringing calamity to each one in turn. The ark was placed in the temple of the Philistine god Dagon in Ashdod, after which we read: "And when the people of Ashdod arose early in the morning, there was Dagon, fallen on its face to the earth before the ark of the Lord. So they took Dagon and set it in its place again. And when they arose early the next morning, there was Dagon, fallen on its face to the ground before the ark of the Lord. The head of Dagon and both the palms of its hands were broken off on the threshold; only Dagon's torso was left of it" (1 Samuel 5:3–4).

This was a sign of things to come, for we then read: "But the hand of the Lord was heavy on the people of Ashdod, and He ravaged them and struck them with tumors" (1 Samuel 5:6). By this time, the inhabitants of Ashdod had had quite enough of the ark and passed it on to the next Philistine city. Once again, its inhabitants were tormented by tumors, until finally they decided to send it back to the Israelites.

The Hebrews rejoiced to see the ark returning to them. It was pulled across the fields of Bethshemesh on an ox-drawn cart. However, the sacredness and mysterious powers of the ark would soon be impressed upon the Israelites. When a clan of Israelites known as the descendants of Jeconiah refused to celebrate the return of the ark, 70 of them were struck down.

Years later, when David became king, he brought the ark up to Jerusalem. On the way, Uzzah "put out his hand to the ark of God and took hold of it, for the oxen stumbled. Then the anger of the Lord was aroused against Uzzah; and God struck him there for his error; and he died there beside the ark of God" (2 Samuel 6:6–7).

We read that David was angered because the Lord struck down Uzzah. The divine action can perhaps only be understood as emphasizing the holiness of God, before whom no man can stand. Apparently, Uzzah disregarded one very important command from God: to respect the sanctity of the ark and never to touch it.

After this incident, David was reluctant to bring the ark to Jerusalem, and for three months the ark was entrusted to the care of Obed-edom the Gittite.

Solomon, David's successor, placed the ark within the Holy of Holies of his temple. At this point, the ark was said to contain Aaron's rod that budded and a pot of manna, along with the Ten Commandments. Hovering over the ark in the darkness of the Holy of Holies were two golden cherubim, their solitude disturbed only by the annual appearance of the High Priest.

Most scholars believe the ark of the covenant was captured or destroyed by the Babylonians when Jerusalem fell in 586 B.C. Some believe that this mysterious object was not destroyed but remains in a secret location, ready to be revealed at the ordained time.

The Search for the Ark

he 1981 film *Raiders of the Lost Ark* popularized the search for the ark of the covenant. Interestingly, one premise of the movie—that the ark was taken by Pharaoh Shishak in the tenth century B.C.—has been superseded by other increasingly popular views.

According to Jewish tradition, at the time of the fall of Jerusalem in 586 B.C., the prophet Jeremiah "commanded the tabernacle and the ark to go with him, as he went forth into the mountain, where Moses climbed up, and saw the heritage of God. And when [Jeremiah] came thither, he found an hollow cave, wherein he laid the tabernacle, and the ark, and the altar of incense, and so stopped the door" (2 Maccabees 2:4–5, KJV).

Moses died on Mount Nebo in Transjordan. When some of his followers attempted to mark the location, Jeremiah rebuked them: "As for that place, it shall be unknown until the time that God gather his people again together, and receive them unto mercy" (2 Maccabees 2:7). Investigators have scoured Mount Nebo in hopes of finding the ark, but thus far their efforts have been fruitless.

Some believe the ark was hidden near the ancient settlement of Qumran by the Dead Sea. The excavation of numerous caves has proved fruitless. Still others suggest a number of sites in Jerusalem, including a tunnel at Gordon's Calvary, the possible site of the crucifixion of Christ.

Many Jews believe the ark is hidden in a secret chamber carved deep under the Temple Mount. It is thought that King Solomon foresaw a time when the ark would need to be hidden, and he carved out an underground chamber.

In the 1980s, orthodox rabbis were building a synagogue adjoining the western retaining wall of the so-called Second Temple (built by King Herod) when they broke through a subterranean gate. They discovered a hall leading in the direction of the area thought to be the Holy of Holies.

The rabbis proceeded with their clandestine excavation cautiously, fearing that the Muslims controlling the Temple Mount above them would demand an end to their digging. After 18 months of these secret excavations, the passageway ended at a sealed wall. The rabbis were convinced that somewhere on the other side lay the Holy of Holies and the ark of the covenant.

At this point, Muslim authorities learned of the excavation. A riot was narrowly averted, and the Israeli government forced the rabbis to end their excavations and seal up the tunnel.

The rabbis remain convinced that the ark of the covenant lies somewhere deep beneath the Temple Mount and that it will be brought to light one day when, as 2 Maccabees states, "God gather his people again together, and receive them unto mercy."

Ancient Israel

eferences to ancient Israel outside the Bible are few. One mention that has been of considerable interest to scholars is an inscription found in an Egyptian temple at the end of the last century. It sheds light on one of the most important events in Israel's early history.

The date of the Exodus and the Israelites' conquest of Canaan has been fiercely debated among scholars. One popular theory is that the biblical portrayal is an exaggerated account of what was actually a gradual process during which the Israelites emerged from peoples indigenous to Canaan.

According to this theory, the dramatic stories of the conquest of Jericho and other cities are merely religiously motivated fables with little historical basis. The development of the Israelite nation supposedly took place in the middle of the 12th century B.C.—around 1150 B.C. That is more than 200 years later than the Bible says the conquest of Canaan took place.

In 1896, the great Egyptologist Flinders Petrie was excavating in the mortuary temple of Pharaoh Merneptah in Thebes when he discovered what has become known as the Merneptah Stela. A stela is a cut, standing stone with writing on it, used in ancient times to chronicle important events in the reign of a king or pharaoh.

The Merneptah Stela preserves what is the most important mention of Israel outside the Bible and the only mention of Israel in Egyptian records. The stela is, in fact, a poetic eulogy to Merneptah, who ruled after Ramses the Great, from 1212 B.C. to 1202 B.C. At the end of the poem is a record of Merneptah's military campaign into Canaan around 1210 B.C. It is here that we find this citation: "Israel is laid waste, its seed is not."

This text poses a problem for the so-called gradual emergence theory, for it suggests that Israel was already a recognizable entity by 1210 B.C., instead of 1150 B.C. or later. Accordingly, the Merneptah Stela has been carefully analyzed by scholars in an attempt to harmonize it with the gradual emergence theory. It has been suggested that the word *Israel* actually refers to "Jezreel," the valley in the north of the country, or perhaps to the Libyans— "the wearers of the side lock."

These alternative renderings have not met with widespread acceptance. The word for Israel is accompanied in the Merneptah Stela with a special hieroglyphic indicator for "people," not a geographic feature, such as a valley. The presence of Israel in a list of Canaanite peoples argues against identifying it with Libya.

Attention has also focused on the meaning of the word *seed* as it appears in the stela. There are only two possibilities: "grain" or "offspring." But a comparison with the use of the same term in other Egyptian texts affirms that it refers to grain.

It would be unwise to attempt to draw too much from this overly scrutinized text. The evidence does show that, in the 13th century B.C., a nation named Israel existed and was an important enough military power to be mentioned on the stela.

It also seems clear from the reference to grain that the Israelites were primarily agrarian. The biblical text supports the fact that during this period the Israelites did not occupy fortified city-states but were primarily tillers of the soil. Grain storage pits are common in the hill country sites that they occupied.

The examination of teeth from tombs of the period also indicates that grain was a primary food source. The worn state of the teeth is due to the fact that stone mills were used to grind the grain, which would therefore contain minute particles of stone.

The debate over the date of the Exodus and the conquest of Canaan continues, and this latest research will surely give biblical scholars something more to chew on.

Fire and Rain

rouble visited Israel when King Ahab married a Sidonian princess by the name of Jezebel. The meaning of her name, "Baal is the prince," foreshadows the fierce struggle that her reign would initiate between the god Baal and Yahweh, the God of the Israelites.

The crafty Jezebel sought to replace the prophets in Israel with prophets of Baal and his consort Asherah. Baal's name means "lord" or "owner," and he was revered as the supreme deity of Canaan. He was also worshiped by the Phoenicians, the Philistines, and other peoples of the region (hence the various derivatives of Baal mentioned in the Bible, including the Philistine Baal-Zebub, or "lord of the flies"; the Moabite Baal-Meon, or "lord of the residence"; and Baal-Gad, "the lord of Gad" of Lebanon).

Baal was a storm-god who was believed to send the rains in their seasons. His entourage included rain clouds, and lightning was his weapon. Baal worship was a great temptation for the water-poor land of Israel. Unlike the great river cultures of Egypt and Mesopotamia, Israel had no constant supply of water and was thus dependent upon the winter rains to sustain its crops.

In return for supplying rain, Baal was thought to demand submission in the form of human sacrifice. In the Bible, this form of sacrifice is termed "to pass through the fire." As the phrase suggests, the victims were burned alive, and such sacrifice was given as a primary cause for the fall of the kingdom of Israel: "And they caused their sons and daughters to pass through the fire, practiced witchcraft and soothsaying, and sold themselves to do

evil in the sight of the Lord, to provoke Him to anger" (2 Kings 17:17).

The misery and degradation that Baal worship threatened to bring

The test of Baal's prophets

upon Israel prompted the courageous prophet Elijah to confront the prophets of Baal. Elijah challenged King Ahab to assemble on Mount Carmel "the four hundred and fifty prophets of Baal, and the four hundred prophets of Asherah, who eat at Jezebel's table" (1 Kings 18:19).

Episodes surrounding Elijah take up more of the books of Kings (1 Kings 17:1–2 Kings 2:25) than those of any other person except for Solomon.

Despite the odds, Elijah confidently proclaimed to all those present: "How long will you falter between two opinions? If the Lord is God, follow Him; but if Baal, follow him" (1 Kings 18:21). The people, however, "answered him not a word."

Undeterred, Elijah ordered an altar to be built, after which the prophets of Baal would call upon their god to send down fire to consume a sacrificial bull; this seems to be a reasonable request to make of a god depicted with a lightning bolt in his clenched fist. We read that the prophets of Baal danced around the altar crying, "O Baal, answer us!" without success. At noon, Elijah could not resist mocking them: "Cry aloud, for he is a god; either he is meditating, or he is busy, or he is on a journey, or perhaps he is sleeping and must be awakened" (1 Kings 18:27).

The earthiness of Elijah's mockery is lost in the English translation. The phrase "he is busy" in Hebrew is a euphemism for stepping aside to a private place to relieve oneself. This enraged the prophets of Baal, and they "prophesied until the time of the offering of the evening sacrifice. But there was no voice; no one answered, no one paid attention" (1 Kings 18:29).

Elijah then prepared an altar, adding a trench filled with water around the altar. He offered a brief yet eloquent prayer, after which "the fire of the Lord fell and consumed the burnt sacrifice, and the wood and the stones and the dust, and it licked up the water that was in the trench" (I Kings 18:38).

Behold the Tunnel!

 any visitors to Jerusalem are awed by the majestic walls of the old city, but they are then surprised to learn that the walls date only to 1537, when the Turkish Sultan Suleiman the Magnificent ordered them to be restored. Even more surprising, no doubt, is the fact that the original Jerusalem stood completely outside the present-day walls.

The Jebusites, one of the Canaanite peoples inhabiting the land before the Israelite conquest, built the first Jerusalem as their capital. The city stood on a low ridge of land extending southward from the present-day city walls.

Though occupying only 13 acres, the city was protected by deep valleys on all sides except the north, where strong defensive fortifications made the city virtually impregnable. Hence the boast of the Jebusites to David: "You shall not come in here, but the blind and the lame will repel you"—because they thought, "David cannot come in here" (2 Samuel 5:6).

The Jebusites did not count on David's men sneaking into the city by night through the water system known as Warren's Shaft. This shaft led to the Gihon Spring, the Jebusites' water source and the main reason they had settled at the site in the first place.

The Gihon is the major natural water source in the immediate area. A copious spring, it flows even to this very day. In ancient times, the Gihon could supply water for a population of around 2,500 people.

Warren's Shaft is only one of three water systems carved out of the rock underneath the Jebusite city, today called the City of David. Solomon carved a second channel along the bottom of the hill where the city stood to provide water for irrigation of the fields in the Kidron Valley through a system of sluice gates. King Hezekiah carved out the third water system.

In Solomon's day, Israel lived securely in peace, and besieging armies did not threaten Jerusalem. Three hundred years later, however, the situation was entirely different. Sennacherib and the

Assyrians had already conquered the northern
kingdom of Israel and were swiftly advancing
toward Jerusalem.

"When Hezekiah [king of Judah] saw that
Sennacherib had come, and that his purpose was
to make war against Jerusalem, he consulted with
his leaders and commanders to stop the water from
the springs which were outside the city; and they
helped him" (2 Chronicles 32:2–3).

Solomon's system of sluice gates may have given
the impression of several springs in the Kidron
Valley—here called "wadi"—but in reality they
all were connected to the Gihon. The Judahites
camouflaged the opening of the spring so that the
Assyrians would not discover it and gain access to
the water. This would have posed a considerable
hardship upon an army that numbered more than
185,000 men.

The people of Jerusalem could not content
themselves with stopping up the spring. They also
needed the water. We read in 2 Chronicles how
the problem was solved: "This same Hezekiah also
stopped the water outlet of Upper Gihon, and

brought the water by tunnel to the west side of the City of David" (2 Chronicles 32:30).

By the time of Hezekiah, the city limits had expanded greatly to the north and west—areas that were also protected by strong walls. The Gihon is in the Kidron Valley, which is on the east side of the City of David. By directing the water from the east to the west side, Hezekiah brought it closer to where they needed it—close to the quarter of his expanding population.

How did he bring the water across? The answer was lost until the 19th century, when a passage was discovered deep under the City of David. It led from the Gihon to the Pool of Siloam on the western flank of the city. Until then it was thought that the Pool of Siloam was fed by a separate spring.

The 1700-foot-long water channel was known as Hezekiah's Tunnel. It is an admirable feat of engineering made even more remarkable by the discovery of an ancient inscription written by its excavators. This eighth-century B.C. inscription, now in the Istanbul museum, reads in part:

Behold the tunnel. This is the story of
its cutting. While the miners swung
their picks, one towards the other, and
when there remained only 3 cubits to
cut, the voice of one calling to his fellow was heard. . . . So the day they broke
through the miners struck, one against
the other, pick against pick, and the water
flowed from the spring towards the pool,
1200 cubits. The height of the rock above
the head of the miners was 100 cubits.

One puzzle remained, however. The tunnel is
not carved in a straight path to the Pool of Siloam.
It takes a serpentine, roundabout route, which adds
hundreds of feet to its length. Since they dug the
tunnel in haste as the Assyrians advanced toward
Jerusalem, it seems odd that the engineers would
intentionally complicate what was already a daunt-
ing task.

Some have suggested that the excavators mis-
calculated, resulting in a crooked tunnel, but this
is not likely. Engineers in ancient times were

completely capable of excavating straight channels, as can be seen in the impressive water tunnel at Megiddo.

The inscription found in the tunnel shows that Hezekiah's engineers knew what they were doing. They correctly calculated both the distance and the depth of the tunnel underground.

Recent examination of the tunnel provides the most likely reason for Hezekiah's mysterious crooked tunnel. The evidence shows that the path of the tunnel followed a natural fissure in the rock that wound its way circuitously underneath the City of David. Rather than carve a completely new channel through the hard limestone, the engineers decided to follow and enlarge an already existing crevice.

What seems at first glance to have been a wastefully laborious route was actually easier than attempting to carve a direct route—an important point considering the approaching menace of the Assyrian army.

Is the Ark in Ethiopia?

ne of the oldest and most intriguing theories about the ark of the covenant is that it has resided in Ethiopia for the past 3,000 years. The story is preserved in the Ethiopian royal chronicles and is widely believed by Ethiopian Christians and Jews alike.

According to the chronicles, the Queen of Sheba mentioned in the Bible was from Ethiopia. She had a son named Menelik I by King Solomon. The ark is said to have been secretly taken from Jerusalem by Menelik after Solomon's death.

The ark is reportedly kept in the chapel at Saint Mary of Zion Church in Axum, Ethiopia. Years ago the ark was on view once a year, when it was brought out for a ceremony. Some scholars believe the covered object paraded in Axum during the ceremony was actually a replica of the true ark. The ark is now kept in its chapel at all times, and only the guardian monk is allowed anywhere near it.

The theory that the ark of the covenant is in Ethiopia has serious difficulties. For one, scholars believe that the kingdom of the Queen of Sheba was not in Africa but in the area of southwest Arabia now know as Yemen. Also, it is doubtful whether anyone could have succeeded in removing the ark from the Holy of Holies. Entering the Holy of Holies was almost inconceivable for anyone— even priests; only the High Priest was permitted to enter it, and on only one day each year.

It does not, in any case, appear that the ark was moved at such an early date as the Ethiopian theory requires. There is a reference to the ark during the time of Josiah, almost 300 years after the time when it was thought to have been taken to Ethiopia: "[Josiah] said to the Levites who taught all Israel and were holy to the Lord, 'Put the holy ark in the house which Solomon the son of David, king of Israel, built. It shall no longer be a burden on your shoulders" (2 Chronicles 35:3).

It appears that the ark was still in Jerusalem at a much later time than allowed by those who believe the Ethiopian theory.

An Ancient Fingerprint

e read in the Book of Jeremiah that a scribe named Baruch assisted the prophet: "Then Jeremiah called Baruch the son of Neriah; and Baruch wrote on a scroll of a book, at the instruction of Jeremiah, all the words of the Lord which he had spoken to him" (Jeremiah 36:4). This very same Baruch is the only ancient personage whose fingerprint is thought to have been preserved.

In a remarkable correlation with the biblical text, the name "Baruch" appears on an ancient seal known as a "bulla" unearthed at the City of David excavations in Jerusalem. The bulla, a lump of clay impressed with a seal, was used to secure documents, which in Jeremiah's day were scrolls. They would tie with string and then seal the scroll with the lump of clay to identify the owner.

The bulla found at the City of David is dated to the sixth century B.C., the last years of the kingdom of Judah chronicled by the prophet Jeremiah. It reads: "Belonging to Berekhyahu, son of Neriyahu,

the Scribe." Berekhyahu is the long form of the
name Baruch, meaning "Blessed of Yahweh." The
identification of this seal with the biblical Baruch is
confirmed by the fact that Baruch's father is called
Neriah—a variant of Neriyahu—in the Bible.

The location where the seal was found also
fits with what we know of Jeremiah. The seal
was found near what is known as the "stepped-
stone structure," thought to be a retaining wall for
David's palace in ancient Jerusalem. Jeremiah frequently appeared before the king of Jerusalem and
would have been present in the same place where
archaeologists uncovered the seal.

Another bulla bearing the same name was found;
this one contained a fingerprint on its edge. Since
Baruch would have been the person to use a seal
containing his name, there is little doubt that it is
the fingerprint of the biblical personage Baruch.

In the Book of Jeremiah, the prophet states:
"and I gave the purchase deed to Baruch the son
of Neriah, son of Mahseiah, in the presence of
Hanamel my uncle's son, and in the presence of
the witnesses who signed the purchase deed, before

all the Jews who sat in the court of the prison"
(Jeremiah 32:12).

It was during the signing and sealing of this
document, or another like it, that the fingerprint of
Baruch was preserved for all time.

The Fall of Babylon

he Greek historian Herodotus, sometimes
called the "Father of History," is one of
our prime sources of information about
the fall of Babylon. Herodotus lived a century after
the time of Daniel and traveled widely in the East.

In his *Histories,* we learn of the campaign of
Persia's King Cyrus against Babylon. Herodotus
provides many illuminating details, including
the fact that no Persian king, including Cyrus,
would drink the water of any stream other than
the Choaspes, a river that flows past the Persian
capital of Susa. Wherever the king went, a long
train of four-wheeled mule wagons followed

him, transporting silver jars filled with the river's water—which, curiously, was always boiled.

On his march to Babylon, Cyrus was preparing to cross the Gyndes River when one of his sacred white horses fell into the swift current and was carried away. Furious that the river would dare take one of his prized steeds, he vowed to make it so tame that a woman could cross it without getting her knees wet. Temporarily forsaking his march on Babylon, he marked off 180 channels to be dug on either side of the river. The diverted water reduced the flow of the Gyndes to little more than a trickle.

Having taken his revenge, Cyrus resumed his march on Babylon, where the defenders of the great city were waiting for him. After attacking Cyrus's troops unsuccessfully, they retreated within the massive city walls. Herodotus writes that the Babylonians were well prepared for a long siege, having accumulated enough food to last for years.

The siege of the city seemed to accomplish little. Cyrus was beginning to despair when he remembered his experience with the Gyndes; thus a brilliant strategy was set in motion. The seemingly impenetrable walls of Babylon had one weak point, where the Euphrates River flowed under them on its course directly through the middle of Babylon.

Cyrus stationed his troops near where the river entered and exited the city. He then went upstream with his construction troops to a point where it was possible to divert the river. His men worked furiously, careful not to give themselves away, and soon the depth of the river was reduced so that it came up to no more than the middle of a man's thigh. Cyrus's troops waited until nightfall and swept into the city.

Herodotus reports that, if they had been aware of Cyrus's strategy, the Babylonians could have attacked the invading troops from the walls overlooking the river. Another reason for Cyrus's success was that the people of the city were celebrating the feast of Belshazzar, dancing and enjoying themselves while the Persians entered Babylon by stealth.

A Fateful Night in Babylon

t was a story many scholars considered too fantastic to be true—until new evidence shed light on the last evening in the life of King Belshazzar and his kingdom.

We read in the Book of Daniel that Belshazzar made a great feast for 1,000 of his lords. As the wine flowed, the king was in a boastful mood, and he ordered that the gold and silver vessels that his father, Nebuchadnezzar, had taken from the Temple of Jerusalem be brought out so that his guests could drink from them.

To use the sacred objects for drunken revelry was more than a show of contempt. To those present, the act would be yet another reminder of the humiliation that the Jews suffered in the conquest of their country and the carrying off of their temple treasures.

What happened next put an instant end to the festivities. As the glasses were filled and the gods of

Babylon were praised, suddenly the hall fell silent. A finger appeared and began to write on the wall. No one present understood the meaning of the four words: MENE, MENE, TEKEL, PARSIN.

The text then describes Belshazzar's response: "The king saw the part of the hand that wrote. Then the king's countenance changed, and his

The prophet Daniel

thoughts troubled him, so that the joints of his hips were loosened and his knees knocked against each other" (Daniel 5:5–6). He immediately called for his magicians and diviners, promising the third place in his kingdom for whoever succeeded in interpreting the writing.

The wise men of Babylon, however, were unable to translate the writing. Then the queen suggested that Belshazzar summon Daniel, the prophet of Judah who had interpreted the visions of Nebuchadnezzar years earlier. Hastened to the banquet hall, Daniel told Belshazzar the meaning of the strange words.

The message was one of doom: "MENE: God has numbered your kingdom, and finished it; TEKEL: you have been weighed in the balances, and found wanting; PERES [the singular of Parsin]: your kingdom has been divided, and given to the Medes and Persians" (Daniel 5:26–28). Belshazzar was killed that very night as the Medes and the Persians conquered the kingdom of Babylon.

The traditional setting for this story as told in the Book of Daniel is Babylon during the sixth century B.C. In the third century A.D., Porphyry, a philosopher and opponent of Christianity, challenged the sixth-century date for the book. Porphyry dated the Book of Daniel to 165 B.C., arguing that it described events so accurately that it must have been written after the events occurred.

With the rise of biblical criticism in the 19th century, this view became widely accepted among scholars, who viewed the Book of Daniel as a second-century B.C. Jewish national folktale containing little historical value. The fact that, until the mid-19th century, Belshazzar's name was nowhere to be found outside the biblical text lent support to the later date. Nebuchadnezzar was included in the ancient lists of Babylonian kings preserved by the Greeks. But the name of the last native ruler of Babylon and successor to Nebuchadnezzar was listed as Nabonidus, not Belshazzar.

Then, in 1854, several small clay cylinders were uncovered in the temple of the moon god in Babylon. Only four inches long, each cylinder was inscribed with 60 or so lines of the wedge-shaped cuneiform writing used in ancient Mesopotamia. When deciphered, the writing was found to be a prayer for good health and a long life for Nabonidus, who ruled Babylon from 555 to 539 B.C. The prayer also mentioned Nabonidus's eldest son, identified on the cylinder as Belshazzar.

There was no longer any doubt that Belshazzar existed, but he was identified in the cylinder only as the king's son. The mystery deepened as several other references to Belshazzar were discovered in the following decades, and in every case he was identified as the king's son or as the crown prince, never as king.

And yet there was still something amiss. Legal documents from the sixth-century B.C. uniformly include an oath only to the god and the king. The documents attesting to Nabonidus and his son Belshazzar were the only known exceptions to this standard practice. This implied a unique relationship between Nabonidus and Belshazzar.

Other evidence became known regarding the two men from ancient Babylonia. It seems that Nabonidus was an eccentric ruler who spurned the usual gods of Babylon in favor of Harran and the moon god Ur. Significantly, Nabonidus abandoned Babylon for several years and resided at the distant oasis of Teima in northern Arabia. It was during Nabonidus's absence from the throne that Belshazzar ruled in his stead.

The word for "king" in Aramaic, the language of much of the Book of Daniel, is a broad term that can mean "governor" or "crown prince." This is precisely how Belshazzar functioned as the regent of Nabonidus.

This solution solves another puzzle in the story. We read that Belshazzar promised that whoever could read the writing on the wall would "be the third ruler in the kingdom" (Daniel 5:7). Why would that person be third in the kingdom instead of second—as, for example, had been granted Joseph by Pharaoh (Genesis 41:40, 44)? The answer, it appears, is that Belshazzar was already the second ruler, after Nabonidus. The highest position that could be offered Daniel was that of third ruler over the kingdom.

It seems, then, that the story of Daniel fits well into the setting of Babylon in the sixth century B.C. There is no evidence outside the Bible for the writing on the wall, nor could any be reasonably expected to exist.

We do, however, have one last confirmation of the events of the Book of Daniel in the testimony of Greek historian Herodotus. Writing a century after the fall of Babylon, Herodotus confirmed that

a festival was in progress at the very hour that the
Persians entered the city.

☙——❧

Not Just a Face on a Coin

 fter Cyrus the Great decreed that the Jews
should be allowed to rebuild their temple,
their foes succeeded in delaying the project for decades. According to the Book of Ezra, the
inhabitants of neighboring lands "hired counselors
against them to frustrate their purpose all the days
of Cyrus king of Persia, even until the reign of
Darius king of Persia" (Ezra 4:5).

With the ascension of Darius to the throne,
work on the temple finally began, but not before
the opponents of the Jews made an appeal to
Darius. Ezra contains several fascinating letters
between the various parties and the monarch. A
search of the royal archives turned up the original

decree of Cyrus, which permitted the rebuilding. The issue was settled.

What do we know about this ruler who figures so prominently—if only in the background—of the rebuilding of the Jewish temple? Fortunately, quite a lot. The Persians were skilled at chronicling their history, even though it invariably presented their rulers in a positive light.

Darius, who reigned from 522 to 486 B.C., was the second in a line of succession after Cyrus the Great and his successor Cambyses. His rule of nearly 40 years breathed new life into the Persian empire, which had been fragmented by revolt prior to his ascension.

This upheaval in the empire may be that which is referred to in the Book of Haggai, written during the time of the rebuilding of the temple. "For thus says the Lord of hosts: Once more (it is a little while) I will shake heaven and earth, the sea and dry land; and I will shake all nations, and they shall come to the Desire of All Nations, and I will fill this temple with glory, says the Lord of hosts" (Haggai 2:6–7).

The correspondence between Darius and various parties preserved in the Book of Ezra indicates an efficient administration of the empire, a fact confirmed by history. Darius divided his empire into 20 provinces. He built major roads and established a uniform standard of weights and measures. He has also been credited with issuing the world's first currency. A gold coin known as the daric was stamped with Darius's own likeness, showing him running and holding a spear and bow.

The Persian ruler carefully examined the contention between the Judeans and their opponents, and he paid deference to the decrees of his predecessors. This indicates an empire that observed at least some semblance of a legal system.

Despite his considerable achievements, Darius also presided over one of the worst defeats of the Persian empire, at the hands of the Greeks, at the Battle of Marathon in 490 B.C. The battle marked a turning point in Persian history, after which the empire entered a period of permanent decline.

Josephus

xcept for the New Testament, our primary source of knowledge about first-century Judea is the Jewish historian Josephus. If we believe what he wrote about himself, his life was full of fascinating exploits and adventures.

In A.D. 37, Josephus was born into an established priestly family in Jerusalem. Educated in a rabbinical school, he became an authority on the law by the time he was 14. At 16, he was studying the major Jewish religious groups—the Pharisees, Sadducees, and Essenes—to decide which to join.

Josephus then spent three years in the desert meditating with a hermit. When he returned at age 19, Josephus had become a Pharisee. Seven years of priestly duties passed uneventfully, but at age 26 he journeyed to Rome on a minor diplomatic mission and was shipwrecked on the way.

In A.D. 66, Judea was on the eve of revolt against Rome. Josephus was hardly qualified for military leadership. But—through a series of unusual circumstances—he was appointed commander of Galilee.

Josephus rose to the occasion, leading his men bravely in defense of their fortress at Jotapata. After a two-month siege, Jotapata was about to fall. Josephus and the last of his men hid out in a cave, where they decided to commit mass suicide rather than surrender to the Romans.

Josephus suggested they draw lots, and one by one his men submitted to having their throats slit until only he and one other man were left. Josephus later said that this remarkable coincidence was due either to luck or divine providence.

Josephus convinced his fellow survivor that surrendering would be better after all. They were brought before Vespasian, commander of the Roman legion. Again Josephus managed to save himself. He surprised Vespasian by playing the seer and prophesying that Vespasian was destined to become emperor of Rome.

Curious about this prophet, Vespasian kept Josephus at his headquarters for the next two years, at which time Nero was dethroned and Vespasian proclaimed emperor. Josephus remained in the entourage of Vespasian's son Titus, who completed the conquest of Judea. His presence during Jerusalem's destruction was the basis for his riveting eyewitness account of the siege.

Scholars debate the accuracy of Josephus's account of his exploits during the Jewish revolt. Some of what he wrote was likely intended to justify his own conduct in deserting to the Romans, while cunningly avoiding offending his captors.

After the war, Titus granted Josephus an estate outside Jerusalem. Josephus wisely decided to leave the country, however. In Rome, Josephus was granted citizenship and a lifetime pension, and he was given Vespasian's private home to live in. It was here that he spent the rest of his life recording the history of his homeland, Judea.

In gratitude for the privileges bestowed upon him, Josephus took the family name of the ruling Flavius dynasty as his own, and so Joseph of Matthias became Flavius Josephus.

Who Was in Charge?

 n 63 B.C., Pompey and his Roman legions put an end to the civil war in Judea. That date marked the beginning of centuries of Roman rule, which lasted throughout the period of the New Testament and the early Church. Roman domination came to an end in the seventh century, when the Byzantines were defeated by Arab armies marching under the Islamic crescent.

In the time of Augustus, the ruling emperor when Jesus was born, the Roman Empire had an estimated population of between 70 and 90 million, spread out across much of the known world. All of this required efficient administration, at which Augustus excelled. He established reforms that brought stability to Roman society.

The three major institutions of ancient Rome were the emperor, the Senate, and the army. Prior to Augustus, the emperor and the Senate had often been at odds. When Julius Caesar assumed dictatorial powers, he attempted to abolish the Senate, and its members fled to Greece. Augustus trimmed the

Legions in Judea

Roman legions were not stationed in Judea until the First Jewish Revolt. Only after suppressing the uprising were they permanently stationed in the area.

Legion X Fretensis took part in the conquest of Jerusalem by Titus in A.D. 70. Many fragments of tiles have been found in the Old City stamped with the initials of this legion.

The emperor Hadrian sent legions to put down the Second Jewish Revolt of A.D. 132–135. This revolt was more violent than the First Revolt. Legion X Fretensis took part in that campaign and afterward constructed public works projects. The most enduring of these is an aqueduct extending from Caesarea to springs in the Haifa range; parts of this aqueduct can still be seen today. An inscription attached to the aqueduct reads: "Imperator Caesar Traianus Hadrianus Augustus has made (this aqueduct) by a detachment of Legion X Fretensis."

Legion X Fretensis was apparently aided in this massive construction project by another legion. Not far from the northern end of the aqueduct, an ancient village named el-Lejjun preserves the name "Legion." Another telltale tile stamped with the abbreviation "LEGVIF," for Legion VI Ferrata, was found in this area.

size of the Senate and appointed new members, but he also granted it new powers.

It was not possible to become emperor without the allegiance of the army, yet every emperor was wary of his generals. This proved to be the undoing of many a Roman commander, including Marcus Antonius and Pompey before him.

The Senate now had jurisdiction over one group of provinces, which were closer to home and peaceful. The Imperial provinces, on the other hand, were farther away and required a military presence. In this, Augustus shrewdly kept the upper hand. By directly administrating the provinces where the armies were, he maintained control over that vital institution.

At any given time, Rome fielded numerous legions scattered throughout the empire as needed. Each legion consisted of six thousand men—on paper at least—and was composed of ten cohorts of six hundred men each, more or less the equivalent of the modern battalion. In Acts 10:1, Cornelius is described as "a centurion of the Italian Cohort, as it was called."

The commander of a cohort was called a tribune, one of which (Claudius Lysias) is mentioned in Acts 23. The centurion, an officer in command of a hundred or more soldiers, completed the chain of command in the Roman army. Centurions were usually chosen from among the ranks for their courage and reliability. Several centurions are mentioned in the Gospels and Acts. Curiously, each is presented in a positive light, which is more than could be said about many Jewish leaders.

A Momentous Discovery

he first ancient scrolls at Qumran on the shores of the Dead Sea were discovered in 1947. The search of other caves in the cliffs along the sea was disrupted by war, as Israel and its neighbors fought over the territory where the first scrolls were found.

The fighting and subsequent political uncertainty over who would control the area did not

prevent its native inhabitants, the Ta'amirah bedouin, from engaging in their age-old profession
of hunting for ancient artifacts to sell. Eventually,
pieces of scrolls began showing up in the antiquities market, leading archaeologists to suspect that
the bedouin, who knew the area intimately, had
found other scroll-bearing caves.

In 1952, Jordan's Department of Antiquities
began a search of caves in the area, which led to
the finding of "Cave 3." This chamber contained
fragments of leather scrolls similar to those found
in other caves. Far more important, however,
were the two rolls of copper found in a corner by
themselves.

The two rolls—thin sheets of pure copper—
turned out to be two halves of the same document
into which Hebrew script had been punched.
Scholars were eager to read the scroll, but discovered quickly that it was too brittle to open.

The scholars were at a loss as to how to open
the Copper Scroll. After deliberating for three
years, they decided to send it to England, where
it was painstakingly sawed into 23 sections and

The Most Unusual Sea

The ancients were fascinated by the Dead Sea. We find mention of it in the writings of Aristotle, Strabo, Pliny the Younger, Tacitus, and others. This unique body of water lies on a giant crack in the Earth's surface stretching from Ethiopia to Turkey. At 1,300 feet below sea level, it is the deepest depression on the planet. By comparison, the lowest inhabited location in the United States, California's Death Valley, is 300 feet below sea level.

The water level of the Dead Sea has declined in recent years, and it is now divided into two separate bodies of water. The northern portion is yet another 1,300 feet deep, while the southern end is extremely shallow. The sea is void of all life, except for highly adaptive microorganisms only recently discovered by scientists. It has no outlet, and the evaporation of water through the ages has gradually intensified its salinity.

photographed. Once deciphered, it was discovered that the Copper Scroll is basically a treasure map. The scroll details dozens of hiding places containing fabulous treasure. Scholars estimate the amount of valuables hidden to weigh 58 to 174 tons.

As with many ancient artifacts, the Copper Scroll fared better during the nearly 2,000 years it lay in the cave than it has in the decades since it was removed. The edges have started to crumble, with the worst damage on either side of the cuts.

Intent upon learning the secrets of the Copper Scroll, scholars set in motion the process of decay, which will eventually consume it. Only time will tell if they will ever comprehend the strange list of treasure locations contained in the document.

First-Century Ascetics

he Essenes were a Jewish sect that existed between the mid-second century B.C. to the end of the first century A.D. Essenes were almost all males, and they lived in monastic communities throughout Judea.

The Essenes are believed to have originated in Babylon after the fall of Jerusalem. They reacted against what they saw as the moral laxity of the

Jewish religious establishment and dedicated themselves to the strict observance of the Torah.

Scholars have pieced together the story of how the Essenes came to live in remote areas. Some scholars believe the settlement at Qumran near the shores of the Dead Sea was an Essene community. After the successful Maccabean revolt of 167–164 B.C., some Essenes returned to Judea. They were shocked by what they viewed as the compromise of pure Judaism on the part of the leaders of the rebuilt Temple. Their indignation won few converts, but one of these, who came to be known as the Teacher of Righteousness, was a member of the influential Sadok family, from whose ranks the High Priest had traditionally come.

The Teacher of Righteousness was already favorable toward the reforms that the Essenes advocated when he assumed the office of High Priest between 159 and 152 B.C. However, the hopes of the Essenes were dashed when he was deposed by the Jewish leader, Jonathan. After losing the power struggle in Jerusalem, the Teacher of Righteousness joined the Essenes and soon became their leader.

The Essene Creed

The historian Josephus briefly joined the Essenes. He recorded the vow that the Essenes took before the common meal:

"Before touching the communal food, he must swear terrible oaths, first that he will revere the Godhead, and secondly that he will deal justly with men, will injure no one either of his own accord or at another's bidding, will always hate the wicked and cooperate with the good, and will keep faith at all times and with all men—especially with rulers, since all power is conferred by God. If he himself receives power, he will never abuse his authority and never by dress or additional ornament outshine those under him; he will always love truth and seek to convict liars, will keep his hands free from stealing and his soul innocent of unholy gain, and will never hide anything from members of the sect or reveal any of their secrets to others, even if brought by violence to the point of death. He further swears to impart their teaching to no man otherwise than as he himself received it, and take no part in armed robbery, and to preserve the books of the sect and in the same way the names of the angels. Such are the oaths by which they make sure of their converts." (Josephus, The Jewish War, II, 145.)

Some of the writings of the Teacher of Righteousness were preserved among the Dead Sea Scrolls found at Qumran. He and his followers chose to live apart from Jewish society rather than endure what they viewed as its many corruptions.

From Josephus we learn that the Essenes rose before dawn for prayers. After working in the morning, they partook of a ritual bath. Afterward, they ate their midday meal (in total silence), then worked until evening, when they ate again.

Joining the sect required a probationary period and the swearing of allegiance to the community. Upon becoming a member, the successful candidate was given the emblems of the community: a white robe and belt, along with a tool for digging holes in the earth when he relieved himself.

The law was central to the Essenes. They studied it 24 hours a day in overlapping shifts of ten hours each. They were also preoccupied with the endless copying of biblical manuscripts and the writing of their own religious commentaries.

What Is Anointing?

 he Hebrew word *messiah* means to "smear" or "anoint." The high priest Aaron and his sons were consecrated to the priesthood by being anointed with oil. Saul, the first king of Israel, was called "the anointed of the Lord"—a title that became synonymous with "king."

According to Jewish tradition, olive oil was poured and rubbed on the forehead. The anointing signified that the priest or king was chosen by God and endowed with the Spirit of God.

A transformation took place when the king was anointed. At the anointing of Saul, we read that "So it was, when [Saul] turned his back to go from Samuel, that God gave him another heart" (1 Samuel 10:9).

Through disobedience, Saul forfeited his anointing, and the Lord chose a new king. Samuel was sent to Bethlehem, and after finding David, "took the horn of oil and anointed him in the midst of his brothers; and the Spirit of the Lord came upon David from that day forward" (1 Samuel 16:13).

As Saul still ruled, David was forced to flee. Respect for the one who had been anointed was so ingrained in David that when he had the opportunity to kill Saul, he refused: "The Lord forbid that I should do this thing to my master, the Lord's anointed . . . he is the anointed of the Lord"

Samuel anoints Saul as king

(1 Samuel 24:6).

David's successor, Solomon, failed to rule as a shepherd cares for his sheep. His grandiose building projects and expanded empire required high taxes and forced labor, which violated the requirements of those anointed by the Lord.

The ideal of anointing was not fully realized in any of the kings of Judah or Israel. It would be left to the future Messiah to become the fulfillment of the Anointed One.

A Star in the East

or centuries, astronomers and students of the Bible have pondered a strange celestial event described in the Gospel of Matthew:

> "Now after Jesus was born in Bethlehem of Judea in the days of Herod the king, behold, wise men from the East came to Jerusalem, saying, 'Where is He who has been born King of the Jews? For we have seen His star in the East and have come to worship Him.'... Then Herod, when he had secretly called the wise men, determined from them what time the star appeared.... When they heard the king, they departed; and behold, the star which they had seen in the East went before them, till it came and stood over where the young Child was" (Matthew 2:1–9).

Identification of the star is complicated by uncertainty regarding when Jesus was born, which is estimated as occurring between the years 8 and 4 B.C. In those years, several celestial events took place that may have been the "star."

One theory is that the star was none other than Halley's Comet, which would have been visible in the autumn of 12 B.C. It is thought that the tail of the comet helped to "point" the way toward Bethlehem. However, in the ancient Near East, comets were considered evil omens, not signs of good tidings, as the birth of Jesus was considered to be.

Another explanation for the star was the pos-

The star shines on the infant Jesus

sible sighting of the merging of the planets Jupiter and Saturn near the bright star Regulus. Astrologers in ancient Mesopotamia

The Shrine of the Three Kings

The cathedral in Cologne, Germany, boasts the intriguing Shrine of the Three Kings, which is said to contain the remains of the wise men. Tradition holds that these relics were brought to Milan from Constantinople between the fifth and tenth centuries, and were then given to the archbishop of Cologne in 1164. Superficial tests have been done, and experts do agree on two things: the bones are those of males of varying ages (as the wise men supposedly were) and the cloths that contain the relics are consistent with the known dyeing and weaving practices of second-century Syria.

considered Jupiter to be the "king" planet. Since Regulus also means "king," the nearness of the two would have been significant. Also, Regulus is in the constellation Leo, which is the astrological sign of the ancient tribe of Judah. This conjunction, however, occurred a couple of years after the death of Herod the Great; thus it may have been too late to fit the chronology of the nativity story.

Another possibility was first suggested by the seventeenth-century astronomer Johannes Kepler.

He correctly calculated that three alignments of Jupiter and Saturn occurred in 7 B.C. Astronomers now know that the first one took place in May of that year. This would have been a highly significant event, considering that Saturn is the ruling planet of Judah. Also, the alignment took place in the constellation Pisces, known as "The House of the Hebrews."

Even more momentous was a near-alignment of Mars, Jupiter, and Saturn in September of 6 B.C. This event occurs only once every 800 years.

One final possibility comes from records kept by Chinese astronomers, who reported a new star in the constellation Capricorn in the spring of 5 B.C. This star—likely a nova, the explosion of a dying white dwarf star—was visible for 70 days, appearing several hours before sunrise in the East. However, this location would have been the opposite of Matthew's star, as the wise men came "from the East" and journeyed westward.

The suggested theories for the identity of the star, while intriguing, remain unsatisfactory to varying degrees. Perhaps the star was part of a miraculous event, unrelated to any kind of natural phenomena.

Herod's Tomb

 mong Herod the Great's grandiose building projects was a series of fortresses in
the wilderness. These strongholds were
not constructed to protect against foreign invasion,
for Herod faced few if any external threats. Rather,
the fortresses served primarily for Herod's personal
protection. During his long reign, Herod made
many enemies among his Judean subjects, and the
fortresses were refuges he could flee to in the event
of an attempted coup in Jerusalem.

One of Herod's most impressive desert strongholds is Herodium, visible today as a lone, flat-
topped mountain on the edges of the wilderness
east of Bethlehem. The site held nostalgic value
for Herod. In 40 B.C., Herod's political opponents
in Jerusalem took advantage of a Parthian invasion

of nearby Syria to stir revolt in Judea. Forced to flee for his life with his immediate family, Herod fought a rear-guard battle at the site.

The Burial of Herod

Josephus records how Archelaus attended to the burial of Herod, his father:

"Everything possible was done by Archelaus to add to the magnificence: He brought out all the royal ornaments to be carried in procession in honor of the dead monarch. There was a solid gold bier, adorned with precious stones and draped with the richest purple. On it lay the body wrapped in crimson, with a diadem resting on the head and above that a golden crown, and the sceptre by the right hand. The bier was escorted by Herod's sons and the whole body of his kinsmen, followed by his spearmen, the Thracian Company, and his Germans and Gauls, all in full battle order, headed by their commanders and all the officers, and followed by five hundred of the house slaves and freedmen carrying spices. The body was borne twenty-four miles to Herodium, where by the late king's command it was buried. So ends the story of Herod."

During the fight, his mother was critically injured when her chariot overturned. Fearing that her injuries were fatal, Herod tried to commit suicide but was restrained. Herod and his entourage made it safely to Masada. While his mother recovered, Herod made his way to Rome, where he was proclaimed King of the Jews.

The memory of this battle and his mother's near-fatal accident so impacted Herod that 20 years later he returned to build a fortress on the site. As usual, Herod spared no expense in making Herodium another of his impressive construction projects. To increase the height of the hill on which the fortress was built, he leveled a nearby hill and added the rubble to the base of Herodium.

On top of the artificial mountain, he constructed cylindrical walls seven stories high with four massive towers. The tallest, which served as Herod's private keep, had three levels of living space and soared a hundred feet above the walls. Herodium was equipped with the usual Roman amenities: a bathhouse, a columned hall, and a dining room. On the grounds below, a lavish palace was constructed, complete with a swimming pool and formal gardens.

Of all the sites of his building projects around the land of Judea, it was the barren wilderness setting of Herodium that Herod chose for his burial. Josephus described Herod's last agonizing days, during which he sought relief from his various maladies at the hot springs of Machaerus on the eastern shores of the Dead Sea. He finally succumbed at his palace at Jericho. An elaborate funeral procession accompanied Herod's solid gold bier to Herodium, where, according to Josephus, Herod was interred.

The mystery of where Herod was buried perplexed archaeologists for decades. One candidate for the tomb of Herod was the round tower that served as his keep, but some scholars dismissed this notion because typical Jewish custom of Herod's time stipulated that the dead were not to be buried within buildings used as dwellings.

Archaeological digs in the vicinity of Herodium have been hampered by the tense political climate of the area (Herodium is located in the West Bank, a disputed area). Architect and archaeologist Ehud Netzer was not able to begin excavating Herodium until 1967, after the Six-Day War.

Netzer did not start his work at Herodium with the goal of finding Herod's tomb, but its location eventually became something of an obsession for him. In 2006, Netzer was rewarded for his decades of work when he came upon a special stairwell.

Netzer and his team discovered that the stairwell led directly to Herod's mausoleum. All that was left of the mausoleum was its podium and broken remains. Sprinkled around the mausoleum site were hundreds of pieces of splendid reddish limestone decorated with rosettes. When Netzer's team pieced these stones together, they formed a spectacular sarcophagus—one fit only for a king. In this area, that king could only have been Herod the Great. Archaeologists surmise that the sarcophagus was likely hammered to pieces during the Jewish Revolt of A.D. 66 by Jews who saw Herod as a betrayer. No bones were found; Netzer and his team surmised that the site was also looted during the revolt.

In February 2013, Herod's reconstructed tomb and sarcophagus went on display inside Israel's national museum alongside ancient frescoes uncovered near Herod's mausoleum.

The House of St. Peter?

e read in the Gospel of Matthew that, arriving in his adopted hometown of Capernaum, when Jesus "... had come into Peter's house, He saw [Peter's] wife's mother lying sick with a fever. So He touched her hand, and the fever left her. And she arose and served them" (Matthew 8:14–15).

Excavations at Capernaum have uncovered a number of enclosed dwellings called *insuli,* which accommodated extended families of up to 100 persons. These were large walled areas comprised of rooms surrounding a central courtyard. Archaeologists believe that these may be the *insuli* that housed Peter's extended family.

One of the enclosed dwellings contained a room that was set apart from the others. Dating to the first century A.D., it was the only room at Capernaum to have plastered floors and walls. At least six layers of plastered pavement were found, indicating that the area was well-used over an extended period of time. It is thought that religious gatherings took place in this room.

Not only did Peter write two New Testament epistles, but tradition also says he was the main source for Mark's gospel.

Late in the fourth century, a wall was built around this room. Christian graffiti was found on plaster chunks that had fallen face down from this wall—including the names Jesus, God, and Christ. Liturgical expressions such as "Amen" and "kyrie eleison" were also found, as was the name "Peter."

Interestingly, the presence of different languages indicates that the site was a place of pilgrimage. The Spanish Sister Egeria wrote in 384 that "in Capernaum the house of the prince of the apostles has been made into a church, with its original walls still standing." By the fifth century, an

Peter denies Jesus

octagonal church was built over the site, prompting a visitor to write in 570 that "the house of St. Peter is now a basilica."

That structure was eventually destroyed, and Capernaum lay abandoned until excavations in our time have once again brought the ancient site of Peter's house to light.

The Jesus Boat

n 1986, the Sea of Galilee was at its lowest level in memory. In January of that year, two brothers noticed what appeared to be a boat jutting up out of a mud bar that had been exposed by the receding waters. News reports soon trumpeted the discovery of what was dubbed the "Jesus boat." Archaeologists dated the fishing boat to between 100 B.C. and A.D. 100, declaring it the first ancient boat ever found in the Sea of Galilee. Since water decays wood, archaeologists surmise this boat was preserved because mud had covered it for centuries.

Rising water levels threatened the salvage operation as archaeologists sought the best means of removing the fragile remains of the boat. Using new techniques, they encased the boat in polyurethane and floated it to shore.

The Sea of Galilee boat is almost certainly the same type with which Jesus and his disciples (some of them were fishermen) would have been familiar. Twenty-seven feet long and more than seven feet wide, the boat was built with wooden joints, which was the typical shipbuilding practice of Jesus' time. The boat had been repaired on several occasions, indicating it had seen several decades of use.

In the Gospel story of a storm on the Sea of Galilee, Jesus was likely resting in the hold of just such a boat: "And a great windstorm arose, and the waves beat into the boat...But He was in the stern, asleep... And they awoke Him and said to Him, 'Teacher, do You not care that we are perishing?' Then He arose and rebuked the

Jesus calms the sea

wind, and said to the sea, 'Peace, be still!' And the wind ceased..." (Mark 4:37–39).

Ancient sources indicate that boats of this size had a crew of five, including four rowers and a helmsman. Josephus refers to vessels of this size holding as many as 15 people. Jesus and his 12 disciples would have fit comfortably into such a boat.

There is no evidence connecting the Sea of Galilee boat with Jesus. He or his disciples may have seen it or even ridden in it, however. During his ministry, Jesus lived in Capernaum, a few miles north of the spot where the boat was found.

The Notorious Pilate

p until A.D. 6, Palestine had been in the firm control of Herod the Great, who was succeeded by his son Archelaus. After Archelaus was deposed, Rome was concerned about the security of the land bridge between Africa and Asia. To keep the rebellious population in check, Rome annexed Judea as a province and governed it through a series of praefects, or governors.

The fifth of these was Pontius Pilate, who ruled from A.D. 26 to 36. He came to power at a time when Jews were being persecuted both in Rome and in the adjoining province of Egypt. Pilate wasted no time in taking up harsh tactics, and his actions led to a confrontation shortly after he took office.

Wherever Rome ruled, images of Caesar, known as standards, were displayed in military camps and headquarters. These standards, however, greatly offended the Jews, who believed that such signage constituted idolatry. Pilate's predecessors had

An Inscription to Pilate

In 1961, an inscription mentioning Pilate was found at Caesarea Maritima, along the Mediterranean coast of Israel. It surfaced while an archaeological team was excavating the theater, which was dated to the third and fourth century A.D.

Builders in ancient Israel used materials from ruined structures whenever possible because this saved the trouble of quarrying new blocks. It was one of these recycled blocks that gave us Pilate's inscription. When archaeologists were examining the seats of the theater, they turned one of the stone blocks over and found the following inscription in Greek: "Pontius Pilate, Praefect of Judea, made and dedicated the Tiberium to the Divine Augustus."

The word *praefect* (praefectus) is the Latin word for governor. A "Tiberium" is a temple or shrine honoring the Roman emperor Tiberius Claudius Nero Caesar Augustus. The temple mentioned in the inscription has not been found.

respected the Jewish sensibilities and did not display the standards in Jerusalem.

Josephus relates how Pilate, intent upon demonstrating his authority, had the standards secretly brought to Jerusalem under cover of darkness. When the Jews discovered the standards the next morning, the city erupted into riots. A huge mob rushed to Pilate's headquarters in Caesarea and demanded that the standards be removed. When he refused, the crowd staged a sit-in around his residence.

The next day, Pilate summoned the crowd to the stadium, where he had the Jews surrounded by soldiers and threatened with death unless they ceased their protests. At his nod, the soldiers drew their swords to prove that Pilate meant business. To Pilate's amazement, instead of yielding to his ultimatum, the Jews fell to the ground and bared their necks, saying they preferred to die rather than see their law trampled on.

The Jews won that round. Pilate ordered the removal of the standards from Jerusalem. But there would be other tests of will between Pilate and his unwilling subjects.

Josephus records that Pilate stirred up further trouble by taking funds from the Temple treasury to build an aqueduct. This time, when the Jews protested, Pilate was better prepared. He had his soldiers dress in civilian clothing and mix with the crowd that gathered outside his residence in Jerusalem. When he gave the signal, they took out their weapons and killed many of the protesters.

Each of the four Gospels has numerous references to Pontius Pilate and his role in the trial and crucifixion of Jesus. It is surprising, given his dislike for the Jews, that Pilate agreed with their demand that Jesus be put to death. The Gospels record his uncertainty: "You have brought this Man to me, as one who misleads the people. And indeed, having examined Him in your presence, I have found no fault in this Man concerning those things of which

Jesus before Pilate

you accuse Him" (Luke 23:14).

Another crisis brought Pilate's rule to an end. This time he cruelly attacked a group of Samaritan worshippers who had gathered on Mount Gerizim, supposing them to be preparing a revolt. The Samaritans complained to Pilate's immediate superior, Vitellius, governor of Syria, and Pilate was ordered to give an account in Rome. Few mourned his leaving, and with that he disappeared from history.

The Secret of the Cross

rucifixion was a brutal form of capital punishment used by the Romans as a deterrent against the most serious crimes and to keep rebellious provinces in check. The Jewish historian Josephus called it the "most wretched of deaths." To make an example of the victim, a highly visible site was chosen for crucifixions.

Sentences were typically carried out immediately after being pronounced. Upon arriving at the site of crucifixion, the condemned was stripped, flogged, then placed on the ground and roped or nailed to the crossbar, which was then lifted into place on the center post.

The design of the cross reveals the true cruelty of crucifixion. In order to breathe, the condemned man had to push himself up on his nailed feet, causing terrible pain. There was a small wooden block or "seat" placed beneath the buttocks to support the weight of the torso.

The crucified person would often hang on the cross for days, expiring slowly as a result of dehydration, exposure to the elements, and the effects of the scourging. Death on the cross often finally resulted from asphyxiation due to the weakening of the diaphragm and the chest muscles.

We read that "they gave Him [Jesus] sour wine mingled with gall to drink. But when He had tasted it, He would not drink" (Matthew 27:34). The meaning of "gall" is uncertain. Some equate it with the hemlock poison that Socrates drank. If so, it was offered to Jesus to put an end to his suffering, but he refused. Others suggest the liquid may have contained opium, given according to Jewish custom.

The Crucified Man

There are nine references to crucifixion in the works of Josephus, but until 1968, no physical specimen of a crucified man was known to exist. In that year, a burial tomb excavated at Givat HaMivtar, north of Jerusalem, was found to contain the skeletons of a young man and woman.

When the young man was examined, he was found to have a nail through his left heelbone, indicating he had been crucified. Scholars surmise the nail was not removed before burial because the nail was bent (removal of it would likely have been difficult).

Scholars have sketched what the crucifixion of the man probably looked like. His feet were likely nailed on either side of the upright post. The man's fingers and wrists gave no sign of traumatic injury, thus indicating that his arms were tied to the cross rather than nailed.

The legs of the man were not broken before he expired. When it was convenient for death to be hastened, the soldiers would break the legs of the condemned man. This made it impossible for the man to push up and gasp for breath, and he would suffocate more quickly. The Gospel of John records that "when they came to Jesus and saw that He was already dead, they did not break His legs" (John 19:33).

The Romans put a placard around the neck of the condemned man on which his offense was written. According to the Gospels, Pilate had an inscription put on Jesus' cross that read: "Jesus of Nazareth, the King of the Jews."

The Jews, however, objected to Pilate's choice of words because they seemed to confirm what the Jews so strenuously denied. Pilate responded to their objection by stating, "What I have written, I have written" (John 19:22).

The Temple Mount

 n Mount Moriah in Jerusalem stands one of the most imposing structures of the ancient world: the Temple Mount. It covers a quarter of the area of the ancient city.

The Temple that Jesus knew was called the Second Temple. The first—Solomon's—was destroyed in 586 B.C. by the Babylonians. In 520 B.C., under Zerubbabel, the Temple was rebuilt on a modest scale. This structure was used until the time of Herod the Great.

Not content to merely rebuild Zerubbabel's temple, the structure that Herod began in 20 B.C. doubled its area. The size of 24 football fields, the Temple Mount was the largest artificial platform in

the ancient world. Such a massive structure required the kind of technical innovation at which the Romans excelled. The lower end of the plat-form, for example, could not merely

The child Jesus in the Temple

be filled in with rubble lest the walls burst from the pressure. To solve the problem, the southern end of the Temple Mount was built upon huge vaulted structures known traditionally—but erroneously—as "Solomon's Stables."

As prophesied by Jesus, the Temple itself was destroyed by the Romans in A.D. 70. The Temple

Mount was plowed, and a temple to Jupiter was built upon the site. That structure is long gone, and the Temple Mount is now dominated by the Muslim al-Aksa mosque and the Dome of the Rock shrine.

The immense foundation and retaining wall of the Jewish Temple have withstood the ravages of time and continue to dominate the vista of the Old City. Tour guides point out the colossal limestone blocks, some of which are 40 feet in length and weigh 40 tons. They were joined so masterfully—without cement—that not even a piece of paper could be slipped between the blocks.

Why Galilee?

 fter the birth of Jesus, his family fled to Egypt because Joseph had been warned in a dream that Herod was about to search for them. After Herod died, Joseph was told in another dream to return to Israel: "Then he arose, took the young Child and His mother, and came to the land of Israel. But when he heard that Archelaus was reigning over Judea instead of his father Herod, he was afraid to go there. And being warned by God in a dream, he turned aside into the region of Galilee" (Matthew 2:21–22).

Other sources explain why Joseph avoided returning to Judea. The story begins ten years earlier when Archelaus began his reign. Archelaus was no more accepted by the Jews than was Herod, and after a brief attempt to win them over, Archelaus resorted to harsh tactics that exceeded those of his father.

The holy family's journey

Not long after the beginning of his reign, Archelaus suppressed a mob protest by force, killing 3,000 people in Jerusalem. Tensions grew as representatives from the elders were sent to Rome to demand that Archelaus be removed.

As Archelaus went before Caesar to defend himself against his accusers, violence erupted back home in Judea. It was the time of the feast of Passover, and an enormous crowd gathered in Jerusalem—not to celebrate the feast, but to seize control of the city in protest of Archelaus's rule.

As revolt spread across the land, Quinctilius Varus, the Roman legate of Syria, came swiftly with three powerful legions to restore order. After a series of pitched battles, Judea was again subdued. In retribution, Varus crucified 2,000 of the rebels. These events were taking place when Joseph was returning from Egypt. He wisely decided to skirt the troubles in Judea, settling instead in the Galilean village of Nazareth.

Archelaus survived this test of his authority, but he continued to exercise brutality toward his opponents. In his ninth year, after further emissaries were sent to Rome to demand his removal, Archelaus was banished to Vienne in Gaul. Thus began the age of direct Roman rule in Judea.

The Disciples

fter his resurrection, Jesus gave his disciples the following mandate: "Go therefore and make disciples of all the nations, baptizing them in the name of the Father and of the Son and of the Holy Spirit, teaching them to observe all things that I have commanded you" (Matthew 28:19–20).

This command was carried out with amazing speed as the disciples preached the Gospel throughout the known world. While fulfilling their mission, many of the original disciples gave their lives for their faith.

Jesus foretold how Peter's life would end: "Most assuredly, I say to you, when you were younger, you girded yourself and walked where you wished; but when you are old, you will stretch out your hands, and another will gird you and carry you where you do not wish" (John 21:18).

The New Testament reveals that the final journeys of the Apostles Peter and Paul were to Rome, where they suffered imprisonment and death. In his first epistle, written from the Roman capital, Peter relates that he was "a witness of the sufferings of Christ, and also a partaker of the glory that will be revealed" (1 Peter 5:1).

Writing to his close friend Timothy, Paul reveals his private thoughts about his coming martyrdom: "For I am already being poured out as a drink offering, and the time of my departure is at hand. I have fought the good fight, I have finished the race, I have kept the faith. Finally, there is laid up for me the crown of righteousness, which the Lord, the righteous Judge, will give to me on that Day. . . (2 Timothy 4:6–8).

The early Church father Eusebius confirms that Peter and Paul died at the hands of Nero around the time of the infamous fire in A.D. 64, which consumed much of the city. When Peter was told he was to be crucified, the same punishment as was given to Jesus, he said he was unworthy and asked to be crucified upside down. According to ancient sources mentioned by Eusebius, the tombs of Peter and Paul were located on the Vatican hill, under what is now the Basilica of St. Peter.

Jesus and the disciples at the Last Supper

We learn from Polycarp of Smyrna, who knew the Apostle John, that the "beloved disciple" lived at Ephesus in Asia Minor until the time of the Emperor Trajan (A.D. 98–117). He is said to have continued being a witness for the Christian faith, teaching and, on one occasion, raising a man from the dead. The Church father Tertullian, who lived from the middle of the first century until well into the second, mentions that John was eventually taken to Rome and cast into a cauldron of boiling oil, only to escape without harm.

James, the son of Zebedee, was said to be the first martyred disciple, put to death by Herod Agrippa in A.D. 44. However, in other accounts, James is said to have made a trip to Spain. The

What the Disciples Had in Common

The Gospel of Mark indicates that what the disciples had most in common was that they all had glaring weaknesses. They all abandoned Jesus when he was arrested. Mark, however, communicates in his account that God works through all sorts of people. The one who was born in a stable does not call rabbis, lawyers, or kings. Rather he calls those who are weak and yet who seek to be faithful, even in their imperfection.

alleged place of his burial there was a major pilgrimage site during the Middle Ages.

James, the brother of Jesus, remained in Jerusalem. Josephus states that he was stoned to death in A.D. 62. Eusebius claims he was thrown from the pinnacle of the Temple, then clubbed to death.

Other disciples went everywhere preaching the Gospel message. We know, for example, that Mark went to Alexandria and that Thaddeus went to Edessa, in what is now Turkey.

Perhaps the most intriguing story is that of Thomas. The apocryphal Acts of Thomas, written in the third century, claims that he founded a church in India. He is alleged to have worked as a carpenter, performed miracles, and to have died a martyr's death. To this day, a unique group of Syrian Christians, known as the "Christians of St. Thomas," exist among a population that is only 3 percent Christian. They live in Malabar, on the southwest coast of India, and claim to be the descendants of those converted by the apostle. Thomas was reportedly buried near Madras. Modern scholars of Christian church history have confirmed this with a high degree of probability.

Pax Romana

or much of Rome's history, the Pax Romana ("Roman peace") was more a vision than a reality. Rome was often threatened militarily or plagued by political unrest. Rarely was there efficient administration and peace for any significant length of time.

However, one peaceful time was the Julio-Claudian dynasties, extending from before Jesus' birth to the end of the first century. Jesus was born during the reign of Augustus Caesar, who rose to prominence at the time of the civil wars that followed the assassination of Julius Caesar in 44 B.C. Augustus, whose original name was Octavian, gained control over the West while his rival Marcus Antonius ruled the East from Alexandria. In 31 B.C., their armies battled at Actium in Greece, resulting in the defeat and eventual suicide of Antonius.

During the reign of Augustus, the Roman Empire was established; Augustus was the first emperor. He was an efficient administrator who brought many needed reforms to the empire. One of these was to divide the dominion of Rome into Senatorial and Imperial provinces. Senatorial provinces were generally peaceful, while Imperial provinces, which were in outlying regions, usually had rebellious subjects.

Judea became an Imperial province in A.D. 6. The praefect firmly governed it, backed by a strong military garrison. Discontent with Rome was widespread, which led to the rise of such fervently anti-Roman groups as the Zealots. There were no major uprisings until the First Jewish Revolt, which began in A.D. 66.

In A.D. 14, the long reign of Augustus ended with his death, and the throne passed to Tiberius,

Paul in Athens

the son of Augustus's consort Livia. Tiberius continued Augustus's efficient administration. Like Augustus before him, he avoided war by not attempting to expand the borders of the empire.

During this time, the Pax Romana was maintained, bringing distinct benefits to the first evangelists who spread the Gospel throughout the empire. Travel was secure on good roads, parts of which can still be seen today. At this time, Greek was the main language of the Roman world. The writing of the New Testament in Greek made it accessible to every corner of the empire.

An exception in this era of stability was the reign of Tiberius's demented grandnephew Gaius (Caligula) in A.D. 27. There was little mourning when his reign ended. The empire was again in firm hands—those of Gaius's uncle, Claudius. The ministry of the Apostle Paul took place at this time.

Agrippina, Claudius's fourth wife, poisoned him in A.D. 54 so that her son Nero (from a previous marriage) could take the throne. Among the first casualties of Nero's rule were the early Christians. The Apostles Paul and Peter are believed to have been martyred during this time.

With Nero's increasingly unpredictable behavior, Rome's golden age of stability ended. After his death by suicide in A.D. 68, confusion reigned as the throne changed hands three times in one year. Vespasian, the first of the Flavian dynasty, became emperor after his return from Judea, where he had been suppressing the Jewish revolt.

During the rule of Vespasian's son Domitian (A.D. 81–96), the situation for Christians deteriorated.

Trajan, fourth in a line of Vespasian's successors, became emperor in A.D. 98. The Christians had suffered before his rule, but Trajan began the first systematic persecution of the church. Some scholars believe that the persecution described in the Book of Revelation reflects the rule of Trajan.

By this time, however, the church was no longer in its formative stage. Christianity had become a commanding presence despite fiendish opposition.

Ancient Mariners

ince the dawn of recorded history, people have taken to the seas. The earliest references to ships come from Egypt, where as early as 2650 B.C., cedar logs were transported from Phoenicia on vessels more than 170 feet in length. Egyptian reliefs also depict ships being used for military invasions and for ferrying captives.

A tomb painting from Thebes dated to the 15th century B.C. depicts sailing vessels with components familiar to modern mariners: masts with crow's nests, rectangular sails, rudders, and oars.

At the time of the New Testament, the Roman Empire commanded the seas. A relief now in the Vatican depicts a warship propelled by 36 oars on two levels. The ship had an estimated crew of more than 200, with an outside gangway, main deck, and raised platforms for three levels filled with fighting men. With an estimated length of 103 feet, this ship was of moderate size for its time.

Until the development of scuba-diving equipment, our knowledge of ancient ships was limited to references in contemporary literature. Underwater archaeology has revealed the remains of hundreds of sailing vessels built between the seventh century B.C. and the seventh century A.D.

Cargo is invariably found at shipwreck sites. Grain, oil, and wine were common foodstuffs transported by sea. The remains of dried fish, nuts, olives, and pitch have also been found. Unlike the hulls of ships, which eventually disintegrate, the clay jars (amphoras) used as containers for foods and liquids have survived through the centuries.

Shipwrights favored fir, cedar, or pine for the construction of hulls, but they would use whatever wood was available. Because exposure to water decays wood, no large intact ships have been found. However, a few hull bottoms have survived, protected by the sea floor and overlaying cargo. They tell us much about how ancient ships were constructed.

Modern shipbuilding begins with a skeleton. The ancients, however, first crafted a shell of planks. Builders then inserted into this shell a skeleton of frames attached with wooden dowels. This type of strong hull was necessary for the often treacherous waters of the Mediterranean.

Paul on Marriage

 heologians have long suspected the Apostle Paul of harboring a negative opinion of women. They also believe he had a repressive view of the institution of marriage.

But compared to Roman social mores, Paul's teachings were revolutionary.

Up until the time of the emperor Augustus, Roman society had a utilitarian view of marriage, the purpose of which was to produce heirs who would inherit one's property and continue the family name. A husband was fully justified in divorcing his wife solely on the grounds that she was unable to bear children.

In the Roman concept of the *paterfamilias,* the husband ruled over his wife, who was little more than a housekeeper. The purpose of marital relations was not mutual sexual pleasure but procreation. It was common for Roman men to look to prostitutes for sexual satisfaction.

Increasing numbers of men were not bothering to marry at all. Augustus became concerned that the institution of marriage—upon which society was built—was endangered. Accordingly, in 18 B.C. he proclaimed new laws that imposed heavier taxes upon

Saint Paul

unmarried men and women while granting financial benefits to those who married and had children.

After Augustus's new regulations became law, more Roman men chose to marry, but without the intention of entering into a monogamous relationship. Prostitution continued to flourish as before.

Paul refers to this practice when writing to the Church in Corinth:

> Nevertheless, because of sexual immorality, let each man have his own wife, and let each woman have her own husband. Let the husband render to his wife the affection due her, and likewise also the wife to her husband. The wife does not have authority over her own body, but the husband does. And likewise the husband does not have authority over his own body, but the wife does (1 Corinthians 7:2–4).

Paul's teaching here is a radical departure from established Roman customs. It granted hitherto

Paul's Methods

Paul worked as a tentmaker and generally paid his own way, not depending on collections from the congregations he established. Tentmaking was also a great way to meet travelers. If they accepted the gospel, they would spread it.

unknown rights to wives and made them equal with their husbands. His statement that a wife has authority over her husband's body must have been greeted with shock by the typical Roman husband, who had considered himself free to seek sexual pleasure outside of marriage.

Paul's teachings regarding marriage eventually won the day and set a standard for Western civilization that has lasted for more than 19 centuries. While often taken for granted and increasingly challenged, the ideal of a mutual, monogamous relationship in which two people commit themselves exclusively to each other is still reflected in the marriage vows of lands that have come under the influence of the teaching of the Apostle Paul.

Is Peter Buried in Rome?

 o city in the ancient world compared in size or grandeur to Rome. The city was divided into 14 districts and had 265 street intersections.

While the rich lived in villas on the hills of the city, the poor lived in crowded districts in multi-story tenements subject to collapse or fire. Rome had an extensive public welfare system that distributed wheat to most citizens at no cost. Water—which was provided by several aqueducts to the city—was also free and abundant.

Like many modern cities, Rome had become such a melting pot that its citizens complained that Rome was no longer Roman. The foreigners brought their own traditions and found support in their own culturally isolated groups. The Jews would have constituted one of these tolerated underclasses of Rome. Like other foreign groups, they were allowed to build their places of worship.

The names of at least 13 synagogues in Rome are known from ancient sources.

An ancient cemetery has been excavated under St. Peter's Basilica in the Vatican. Both St. Peter's and the original fourth-century church that occupied the site were built in an area that contained pagan mausoleums and other structures dated to the second century (Christians were buried in pagan cemeteries until the third century). Although no bones have been uncovered that might be those of the apostle, the early and continuous reverence toward the site indicates that Peter may indeed have been buried here.

The crucifixion of Peter

In 1953, archaeologist Bellarmino Bagatti uncovered an ossuary in a burial cave on the Mount of Olives in Jerusalem that bore the inscription "Simon, son of Jonah" in Hebrew. Since this discovery, some scholars maintain that there is no proof Peter ever went to Rome (and that he likely died in Jerusalem).

Other scholars believe we may never know where Peter died or where he was buried. Considering the persecutions of Christians that were occurring at the time, his loved ones may have not been able to bury his body. Or, since Christians of the time believed Christ would return sooner rather than later, memorializing the dead may not have been a top priority for them.

❧⸺❧

The Shroud of Turin

cholars and the faithful alike are fascinated by the Shroud of Turin, which some claim to be the burial shroud of Jesus. After decades of analysis, there still is no consensus as to the shroud's authenticity.

The shroud has a colorful history. It has been suggested that it is the same cloth as the *mandylion,*

or face cloth, of Edessa (modern Urfa, in Turkey). The image of Christ was also allegedly displayed on the *mandylion,* which was brought to Constantinople in the tenth century. The *mandylion* remained in Constantinople as late as the thirteenth century, after which it disappeared. Some believe it was transferred to Europe, where it eventually became known as the Shroud of Turin.

The cloth known as the Shroud of Turin appeared in 1355, when it was exhibited in Lirey in northern France. The shroud was partially burned in 1532, but the image was largely undamaged. In 1578, the shroud was brought to Turin in northern Italy, where it resides today in the Royal Chapel of the Cathedral of St. John.

Even though the shroud was exhibited frequently during the late medieval and Renaissance periods, it was never officially proclaimed to be Jesus' burial cloth. To the contrary, many pronouncements exhibited caution regarding its origin.

The first scientific indication of the unusual nature of the shroud came in 1898, when it was photographed with glass-plate negatives. It was discovered that the image on the plate was a positive, an anomaly that, if faked, was produced hundreds of years before the invention of photography.

In 1973, European scientists were permitted to inspect the shroud in order to recommend how best to preserve it. The scientists were divided in their opinions concerning its authenticity. This was the beginning of the Shroud of Turin Research Project (STURP), involving more than 30 researchers.

The first problem that the STURP team tackled was the alleged bloodstains on the shroud. Specialists had been unable to confirm that the stains were blood. However, two experts on the STURP team concluded that the stains were blood. Some continued to disagree, claiming that the alleged bloodstains are iron-oxide pigment.

It has also been pointed out that the bright-red color of the bloodstains suggests they are of relatively recent origin. Others, however, point out that the shroud may have been washed with soapwart, a plant used as a detergent in antiquity. Soapwart has a preserving effect upon blood cells.

In the 1980s, investigators found calcium carbonate (limestone) particles on the shroud. Microscopic examination revealed that the particular type of limestone was not the more common calcite, but travertine argonite from springs.

Argonite is the type of limestone common to Judea, so investigators decided to obtain limestone samples from ancient tombs in Jerusalem. Both the limestone particles on the shroud and the samples from Jerusalem tombs were tested by a device called a high-resolution scanning ion microprobe.

The graphs produced by the microprobe revealed that the samples were a close match, indicating that the shroud had at one time been in a Jerusalem tomb. This positive evidence was seemingly overturned in 1988, when a few pieces of thread from the shroud were tested by carbon–14 dating. Three laboratories, working independently, arrived at a date of origin between 1260 and 1390. These findings seemed to confirm the theory that the shroud was created around 1350 by Geoffrey de Charny, a French knight who hoped to attract pilgrims to his church.

The mystery of the shroud continued, however, as other researchers pointed out that the image itself contains extraordinarily precise physical details that only the most accomplished medieval artist could have attained. In addition, there are no brushstrokes or pigments visible on the surface of the shroud, indicating that the linen was not painted.

The carbon–14 dating of the shroud has been challenged on the basis of new research. Scientists have discovered that various microbes can cover ancient artifacts with plasticlike coatings that significantly alter the results of carbon–14 analysis. That, combined with the minuscule amount of fabric tested, increased the possibility that the initial carbon–14 test results were invalid.

What seems clear is that the image of a man estimated to be just under six feet tall, weighing 175 pounds, and between the ages of 30 and 35 has been inexplicably imprinted on the surface of fabric. While the faithful and the skeptics continue to disagree concerning whose image it may be, it is hoped that further investigation will someday establish with more certainty the date—and authenticity—of the Shroud of Turin.

☙ ❧

An Evil World Leader

he Book of Revelation tells us that a mysterious evil force will arise at the end of the age: "And he was given a mouth speaking great things and blasphemies, and he was given authority to continue for forty-two months. . . . It was granted to him to make war with the saints and to overcome them. And authority was given him over every. . . nation" (Revelation 13:5–7).

World history is the story of great empires. None of them, however, has dominated the world's political system to the degree described in Revelation.

We read that the Beast will use certain symbols: "He causes all . . . to receive a mark on their right hand or on their foreheads, and that no one may buy or sell except one who has the mark or the

name of the beast, or the number of his name"
(Revelation 13:16–17).

The Antichrist, or Beast, will lead the world in a
final rebellion against God. All the peoples of the
world will bow before the Antichrist: "All who
dwell on the earth will worship him, whose names
have not been written in the Book of Life of the
Lamb slain from the foundation of the world"
(Revelation 13:8).

The Antichrist will perform unimaginable feats:
"He was granted power to give breath to the
image of the beast, that the image of the beast
should both speak and cause as many as would
not worship the image of the beast to be killed"
(Revelation 13:15).

Some biblical scholars believe that the Antichrist
is a symbolic reference to the forces of evil that are
always present in the world. Others conclude that
the passages speak of an actual political ruler who
will one day exercise his power over the world.

Who Are the 144,000?

ohn's vision in Chapter Seven of Revelation has long intrigued students of the Bible:

> "Then I saw another angel ascending from the east, having the seal of the living God. And he cried with a loud voice to the four angels to whom it was granted to harm the earth and the sea, saying, 'Do not harm the earth, the sea, or the trees till we have sealed the servants of our God on their foreheads.' And I heard the number of those who were sealed. One hundred and forty-four thousand of all the tribes of the children of Israel were sealed" (Revelation 7:2–4).

Who are the 144,000, and when are they "sealed"? Some scholars take the number literally. They believe the 144,000 are Jewish converts to Christianity who have evangelized the world.

Others point out that the original 12 tribes of Israel no longer exist as distinct entities. Ten were lost to history during the Assyrian captivity in 722 B.C. The remaining two tribes lost their separate identities after the fall of Jerusalem in A.D. 70.

Some take the figure to be symbolic. The squaring of 12 is seen emphasizing completeness. For these believers, 144,000 symbolizes the faithful who will enter history's final stage—when the forces of evil reach

The battle of the end times

their peak. The "sealing" does not mean they will be spared persecution (indeed, the verse that follows describes a multitude of martyrs in Heaven). Perhaps it symbolizes the promise of eternal life.

Some scholars believe the figure refers to the number of martyrs during the final conflict with the forces of evil. However, a later passage describes a "great multitude which no one could number, of all nations, tribes, peoples, and tongues" who have come out of "the great tribulation" (Revelation 7:9, 14). This passage implies that the total number of martyrs will be beyond counting.

Whether the number is to be taken literally or symbolically will likely remain a mystery until the last days.

Epilogue

 o close this book by writing "The End" would be inaccurate. There is no end to the secrets hidden within the Bible. Nor is there an end to the answers we can uncover; scientists gather new information every day through virtual archaeology, down-in-the-dirt digs, carbon-dating, and other hi-tech methods. Perhaps it is best to end this book by saying . . . Amen.